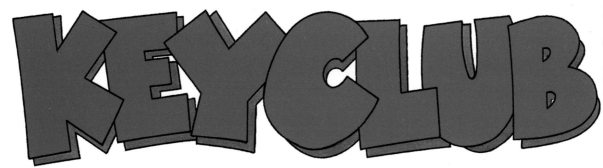

BOOK TWO

by Ann Bryant

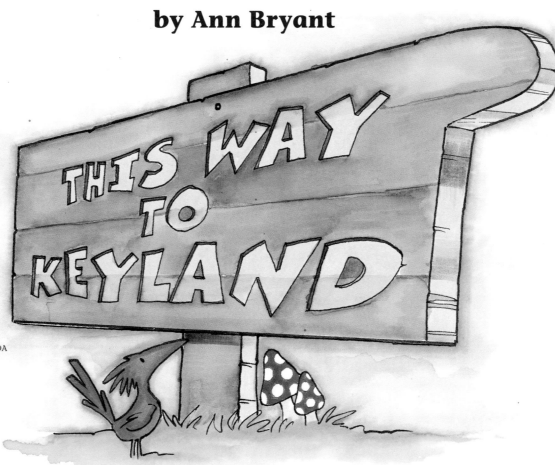

For Jayne Aspinall
Great musician, great friend

Illustrations by
Paul Selvey, John Good Holbrook Ltd.

Design and Typesetting by
John Good Holbrook Ltd.

Music Setting by
Barnes Music Engraving Ltd.

© 2010 by Faber Music Ltd
First published by International Music Publications Ltd
International Music Publications Ltd is a Faber Music company
Bloomsbury House 74–77 Great Russell Street London WC1B 3DA
Printed in England by Caligraving Ltd
All rights reserved

ISBN10: 0-571-53559-3
EAN13: 978-0-571-53559-0

More fun learning the piano...

Hi Keyclub kids, and welcome to Keyclub Book Two.
Just as promised, you're going to find this book packed with exciting things to do and play. Look out for a whole new bunch of great characters and places as you travel through Keyland and have more fun learning the piano.

Where to find what ...

KEYCLUB Kids

At a moderate speed

mf Key - club Kids can en - ter Key - club a - ny time, night or day.

Keys can o - pen doors to pla - ces, and to pie - ces you can play.

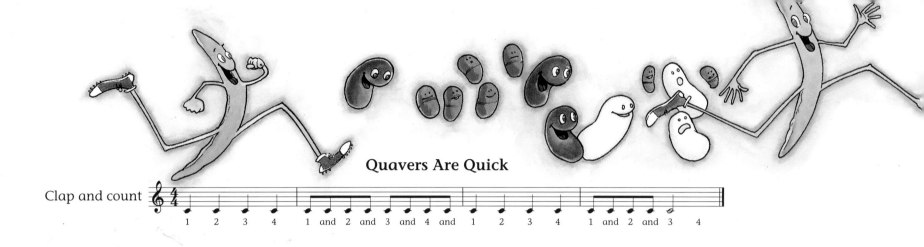

Quavers Are Quick

Clap and count

1 2 3 4 | 1 and 2 and 3 and 4 and | 1 2 3 4 | 1 and 2 and 3 4

Beans Are In!

At a moderate speed

mf

Beans are in! | Beans are in! | Kid-ney, run-ner, broad and but-ter, | beans are in!

Whe-ther they are round or | long and string-y thin, | kid-ney, run-ner, broad and but-ter, | beans are in!

Up!

5

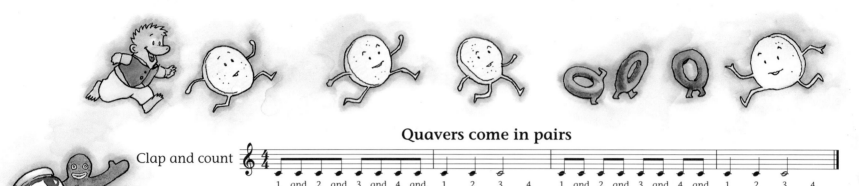

Quavers come in pairs

Clap and count

1 and 2 and 3 and 4 and   1   2   3   4   1 and 2 and 3 and 4 and   1   2   3   4

Clap and count

1   2   1   2   1 and 2 and   1   2   1   2   1 and 2   1   2 and   1   2

Marching Muffin Men

Quite fast

Jaunt - ing | gin - ger breads | jive on the | jam - jars. | Twirl - ing | tof - fee mall-ows | twist and | tap.

Diz - zy | dough-nuts | dance round the | din - ner plates. | March - ing | muf-fin men | rave and | rap. Yeah!

6

Pop, Pop, Pop!

Like a march

mf

Slurp, slurp, slush pup-py, so - so - so - so-da, gin - gin - gin - gin-ger pop, pop, pop!

mf

co - co - co - co-la, vim - vim - vim - to and ju - ju - ju - jui-cy pop, pop, pop!

\> accent

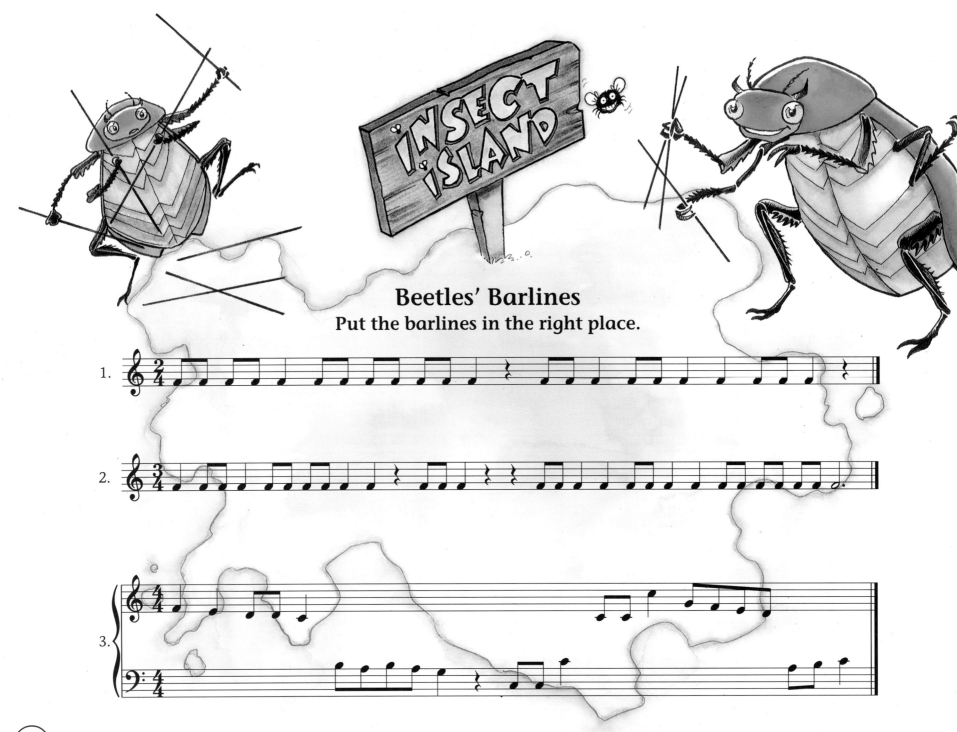

Beetles' Barlines
Put the barlines in the right place.

Tell your teacher the letter names of the notes in exercise three.

The Flat sign

A new note for L.H.

B flat

At a moderate speed

Mac's Afloat

mf

Arm bands and gog - gles and flip - pers and wings, good old

Mac floats a - bout wear - ing hun - dreds of things.

dim.

⑩

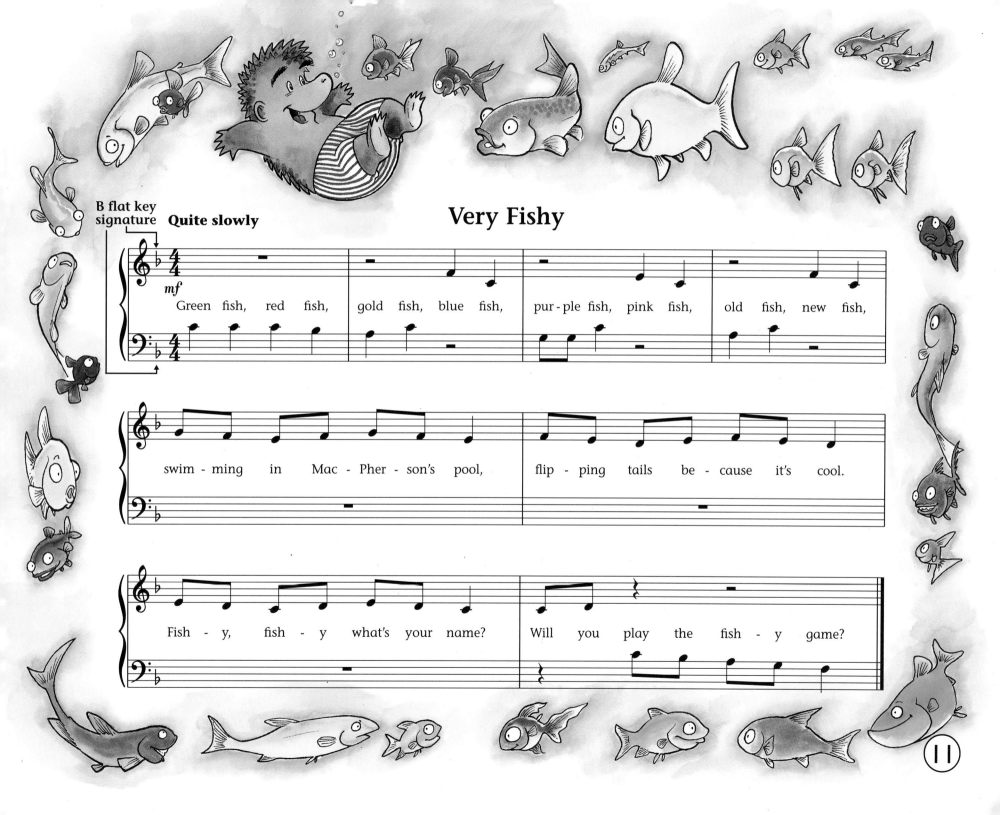

Very Fishy

Water Sports

Slowly

Kangaroo jump

King of the Wolves

Quite slowly

mf
Wil - bur wolf is the king of the woods. He lives a - lone in his lair. If he

hears a sound when he's prowl-ing a - round, his growl sounds *rit.* just like 'Who's there?!'

13

Wilbur in Disguise

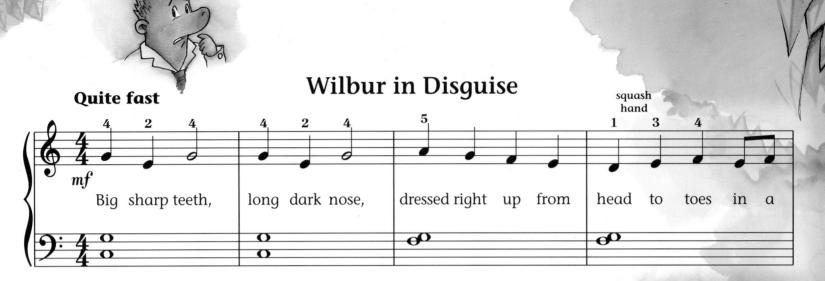

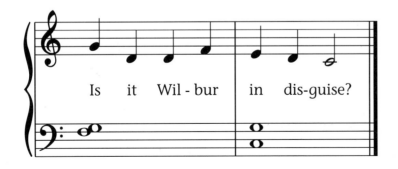

Woodlouse's "What?" Page

What are these? _____

What is this?   >   _____

What is this interval? _____

What note is this? _____

What note is this? _____

What does this mean?   *dim.*   _____

What is this? _____

What is this sign at the start of a piece? _____

What are two notes played together like this called? _____

What does this mean?   **D.C. al Fine**   _____

What does this mean? _____

What does this mean?   *rit.*   _____

15

The Three Bears' House

1st time: **Slow** 2nd time: **Medium** 3rd time: **Fast**

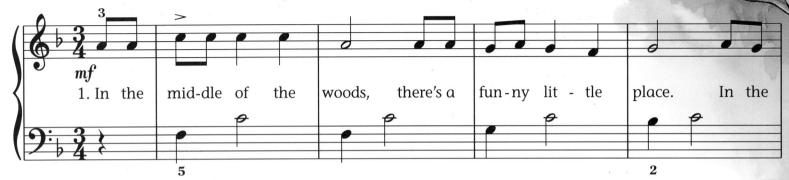

1. In the mid-dle of the woods, there's a fun-ny lit - tle place. In the

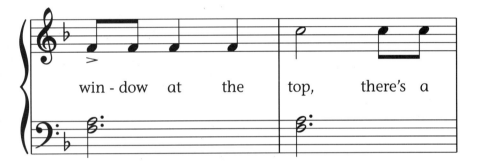

win - dow at the top, there's a

grow - ly dad - dy bear's face.

Verse 2.
In the middle of the woods,
There's a funny little place.
In the window underneath,
There's a smiley mummy bear's face.

Verse 3.
In the middle of the woods,
There's a funny little place.
In the window at the side,
There's a cheeky baby bear's face.

Roly Poly Rabbit

Quite slowly

mf
With a swish, swish, swish and a swirl, swirl, swirl, the leaves all rus-tle when a vole takes a stroll, and the

tree tops sway as the birds all play, and the

dim.
ro - ly po - ly rab-bit tries to hide in a hole.

SUB Soil

Digging and Tunnelling

At a moderate speed

p

Down un-der ground there is | dark-ness all | round, and the | moles | live | there | yeah!

crescendo

Dig-ging and | tun - nel-ling, | dig-ging and | tun - nel-ling, | tak-ing their | turn to keep | watch ev - 'ry | where.

A new note for L.H.

E E E

18

Mole Patrol

Like a march

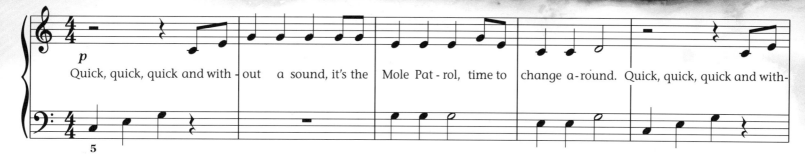

p Quick, quick, quick and with - out a sound, it's the Mole Pat - rol, time to change a - round. Quick, quick, quick and with-

- out a sound, there's a new guard un - der - ground. *f* Up a - bove there are an - gry sighs, as the

Fine

rich black soil spoils the gar - den green. 'One more mole hill and I'll go mad! Such a *crescendo* mess, I've ne - ver seen!'

D.C. al Fine

19

Wayne The Worm

Moles Are Pests!

Terry Tarantula's Transposition

Fill in the missing notes of the piece below so it has exactly the same tune as the piece above, only starting on F instead of C. Look at the steps, skips and frog jump above, and make each interval the same below.

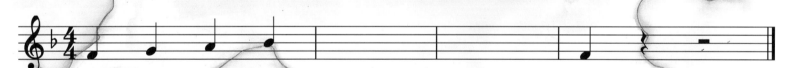

Put a ring around any note you have never come across before.
There should be two (both the same). What letter name do you think they have?
Turn over to see if you are right.

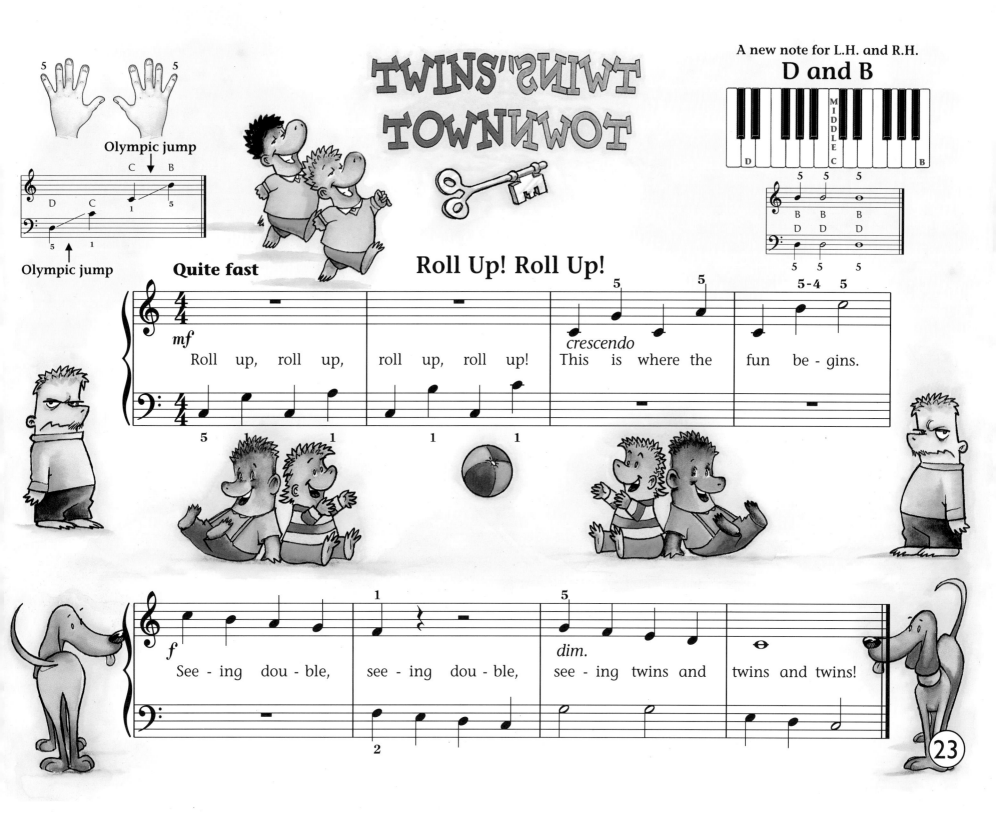

TWINS' TOWN

Roll Up! Roll Up!

A new note for L.H. and R.H.
D and B

Olympic jump

Olympic jump

Quite fast

mf
Roll up, roll up, roll up, roll up! *crescendo* This is where the fun be - gins.

f
See - ing dou - ble, see - ing dou - ble, *dim.* see - ing twins and twins and twins!

23

Dipperty and Dopperty

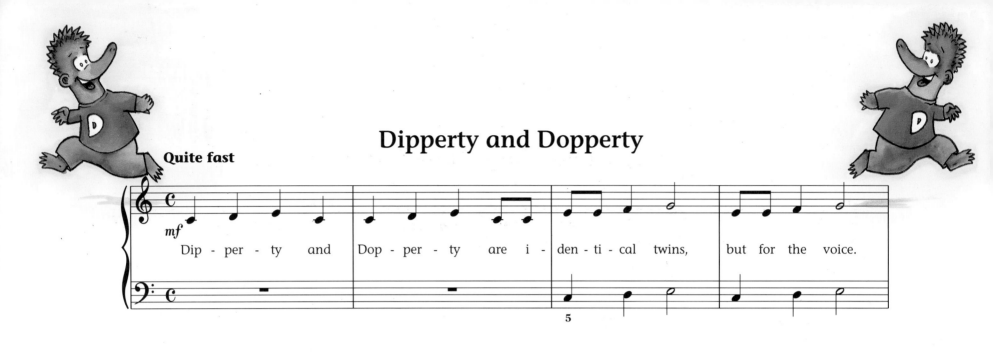

Quite fast

mf

Dip - per - ty and Dop - per - ty are i - den - ti - cal twins, but for the voice.

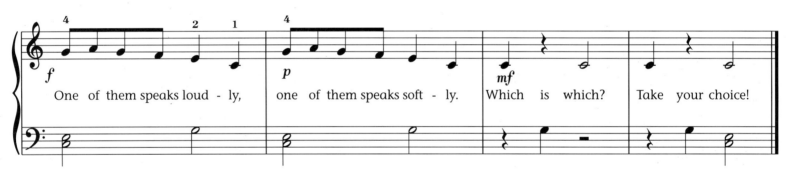

f

One of them speaks loud - ly,

p

one of them speaks soft - ly.

mf

Which is which? Take your choice!

Carie and Mary Quite Contrary

At a moderate speed

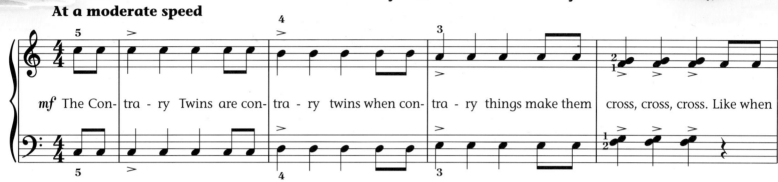

mf The Con- tra - ry Twins are con- tra - ry twins when con- tra - ry things make them cross, cross, cross. Like when

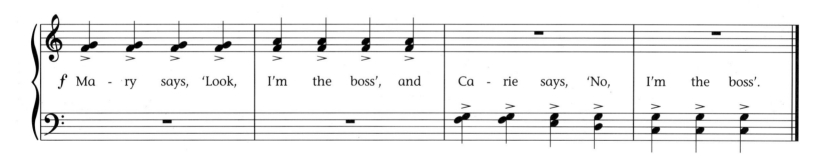

f Ma - ry says, 'Look, I'm the boss', and Ca - rie says, 'No, I'm the boss'.

25

A new note for R.H.

B flat

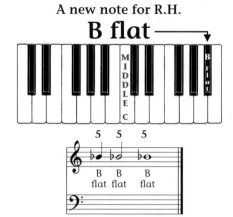

What's the Difference?

At a moderate speed

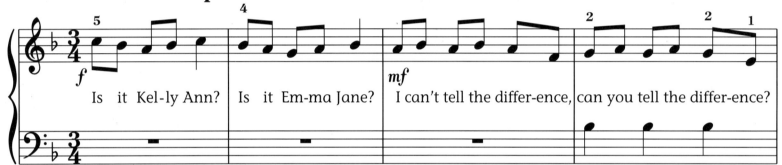

Is it Kel-ly Ann? Is it Em-ma Jane? I can't tell the differ-ence, can you tell the differ-ence?

Kel - ly? Em - ma? *rit.* *dim.* What is your name?

Copy Cats

Notes you know

Intervals you know

Step up

Skip down

Flea jump up

Frog jump up

Kangaroo jump down

Olympic jump up

Rocket

Sky dive

You also know...

dim. or diminuendo - get gradually quieter

cresc. or crescendo - get gradually louder

3 note chord

anacrusis or upbeat

quavers

accent

B flat key signature

28

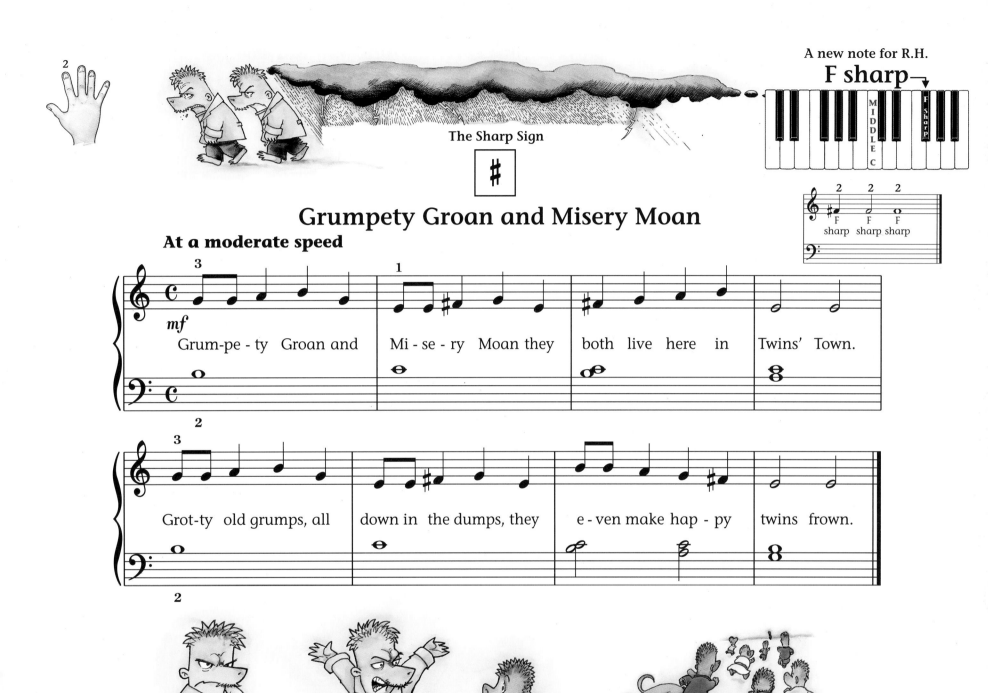

The Sharp Sign

Grumpety Groan and Misery Moan

At a moderate speed

mf

Grum-pe - ty Groan and | Mi - se - ry Moan they | both live here in | Twins' Town.

Grot-ty old grumps, all | down in the dumps, they | e - ven make hap - py | twins frown.

A new note for R.H.
F sharp

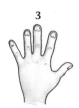

A new note for L.H.

F sharp

F sharp   F sharp   F sharp

3   3   3

Grovelly and Gravelly

At a moderate speed

mf Gro - vel - ly   and   Gra - vel - ly   are i - den - ti - cal   twins   but for their   hair.

One of them has blonde hair,   one of them has black   hair.   Real - ly   weird!   What   a   pair!

30

STICKER HERE

Incy Wincy's Intervals!

Can you write in the correct note to make the interval it says?

e.g.

Skip up

Flea jump up

Frog jump down

Rocket

Olympic jump up

Step down

Kangaroo
jump up

Skip down

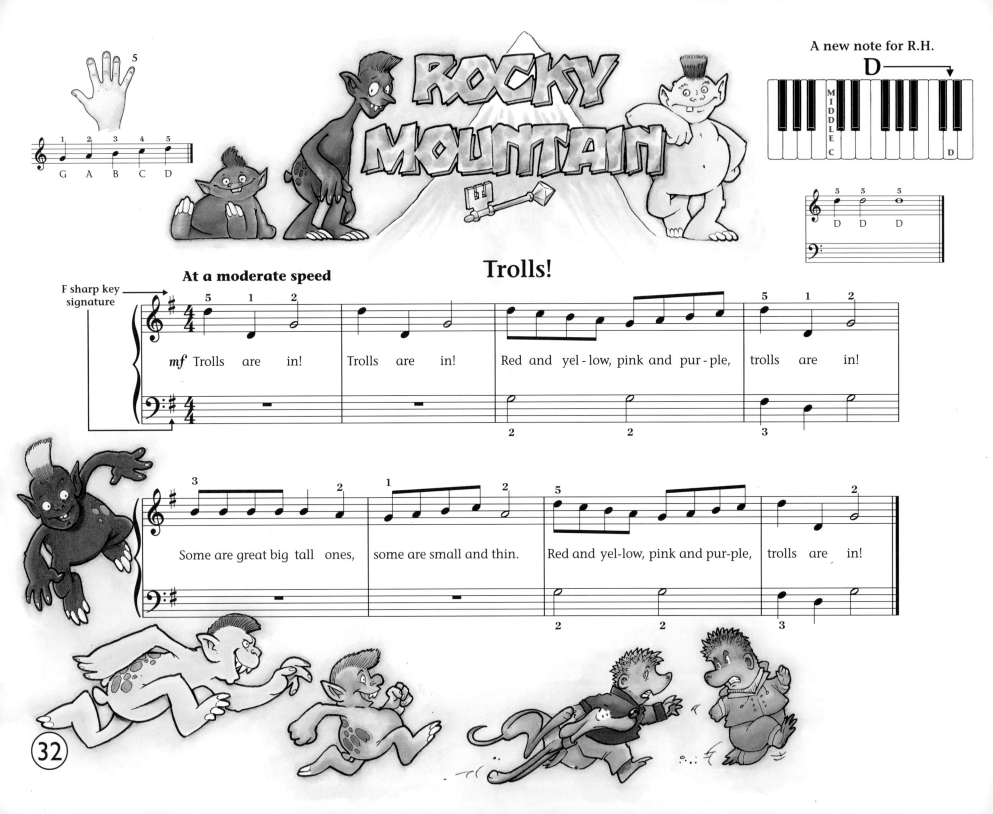

Up and Down the Mountainside

Racing Round the Mountain

At a moderate speed

The Grogs' Grunge Dance

Quite fast

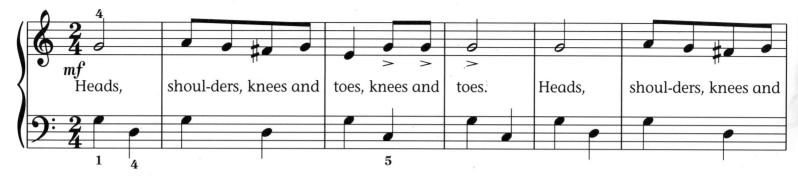

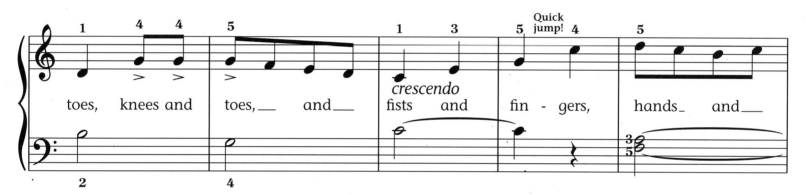

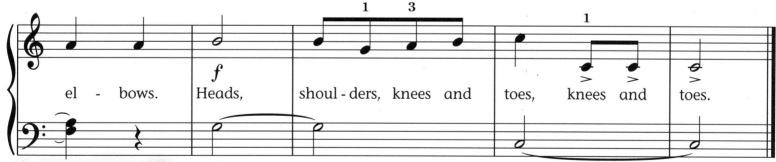

Two More Transpositions from Terry T.

An octave means eight notes apart (like a skydive or rocket).
Fill in the missing notes of piece 2 so that it is all an octave lower than piece 1. We have started you off.

1.

2.

**Fill in the missing notes of piece 4 so that it is all an octave higher than piece 3.
We have started you off.**

3.

4.

36

Mountain Fireworks

At a moderate speed

37

³**D.C. al Fine**

Marvin the Mountain Guide

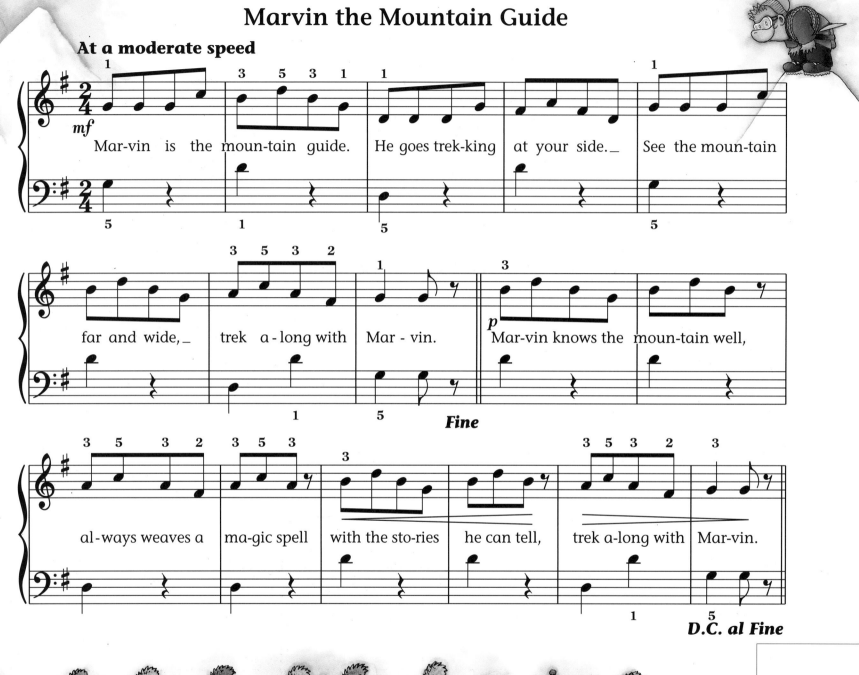

At a moderate speed

mf

Mar-vin is the moun-tain guide. He goes trek-king at your side.__ See the moun-tain far and wide,__ trek a-long with Mar - vin.

p Mar-vin knows the moun-tain well,

Fine

al-ways weaves a ma-gic spell with the sto-ries he can tell, trek a-long with Mar-vin.

D.C. al Fine

STICKER HERE

A Tale to be Told

Slowly and gently

mf Spark-ling with dia - monds and sil - ver and gold, the pal - ace is
ev - ery one knows there's a play to un - fold, the a sto - ry to

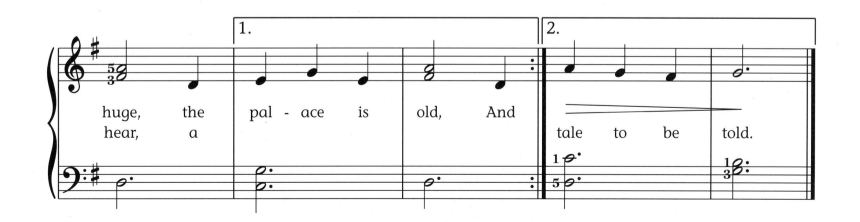

1. huge, the pal - ace is old, And
hear, a

2. tale to be told.

Fairly fast

What A Cheat!

Good old Pete. What

a cheat. Found him a prin - cess and

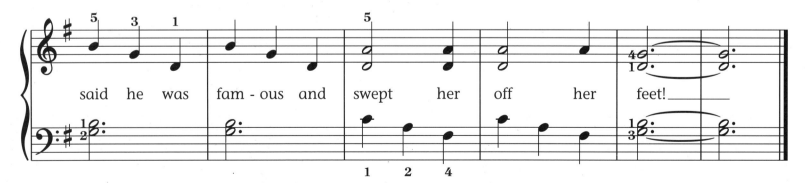

said he was fam - ous and swept her off her feet!

40

Wasp's Words

Make words by writing in the letter names of the notes

Pete - The Roller Blading King

At a moderate speed

Slide, slide, roll-er blad-ing king. Slide, slide,

roll - er blad-ing king. No - bo - dy can beat him roll - er blad-ing

Fine

Pete. No - bo - dy can bring him to de - feat._____

D.C. al Fine

FINISH

2

Pete - Roller Blading Even Faster!

At a moderate speed

Fine

D.C. al Fine

Working Hard at the Palace
(Teacher's Part)

At a moderate speed

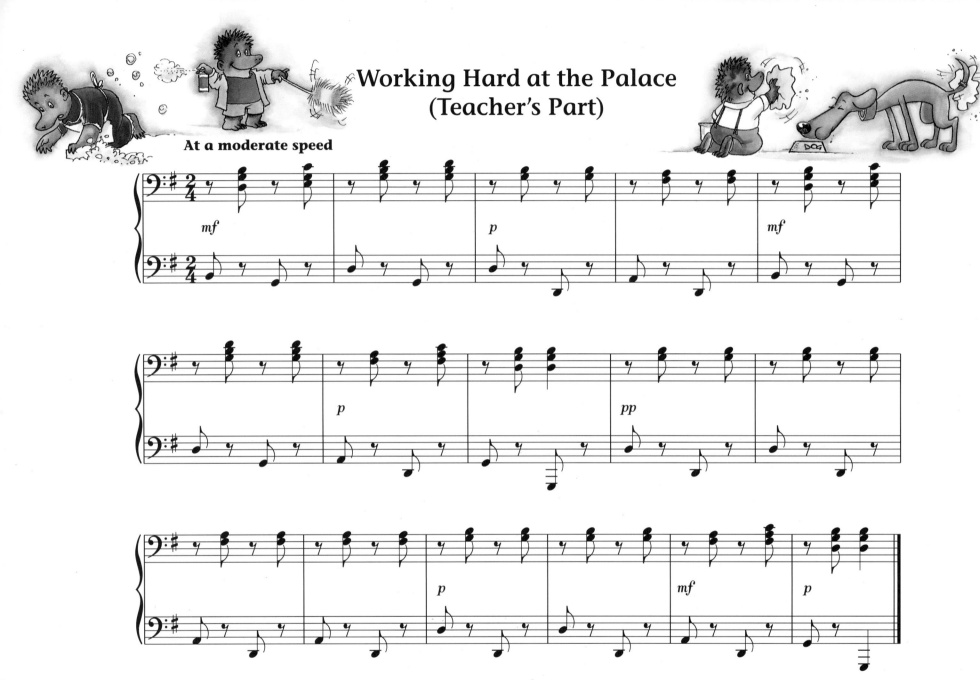

Working Hard at the Palace
(Pupil's Part)

At a moderate speed

INFO-CHECK!

Notes you now know

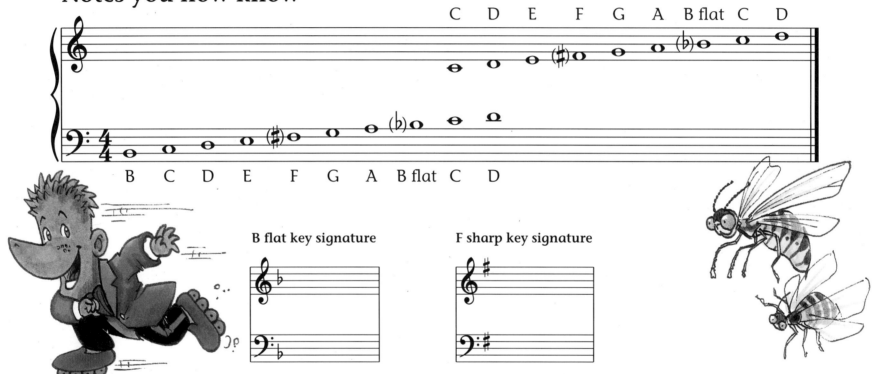

C D E F G A B flat C D

B C D E F G A B flat C D

B flat key signature

F sharp key signature

Intervals

| Step up | Skip down | Flea jump up | Frog jump down | Kangaroo jump up | Olympic jump up | Rocket | Skydive |

46

Time Values

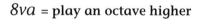 = quavers

Two together make
one crotchet count

♪ = quaver

Half a crotchet
count

♪ = quaver rest

Dynamics or changes in volume

crescendo or ———————— = get gradually louder

diminuendo or ———————— = get gradually softer

8va = play an octave higher

> = accent

anacrusis

47

Well Done!

This certifies that

_____

has successfully completed Book Two
of the KEYCLUB piano course

_____ Teacher

_____ Date